NOR

This book is to be returned on or before
the last date stamped below

100% recycled paper

BLAKE MORRISON

SELECTED POEMS

Granta Books
London

Granta Publications, 2/3 Hanover Yard, London N1 8BE

First published in Great Britain by Granta Books 1999

Copyright © 1999 by Blake Morrison

Some poems in this edition originally appeared in *Dark Glasses* (1984, 1989), *The Ballad of the Yorkshire Ripper* (1987), and *Penguin Modern Poets 1* (1984, 1987), all published by Penguin Books.

A CIP catalogue record for this book
is available from the British Library.

1 3 5 7 9 10 8 6 4 2

Typeset by M Rules
Printed and bound in Great Britain
by Mackays of Chatham plc

Acknowledgements

My main purpose in compiling this book was to make a selection from the poems included in *Dark Glasses*, *The Ballad of the Yorkshire Ripper* and *Penguin Modern Poets 1*, all of which are now out of print. In the process, I've added some previously unpublished and uncollected poems, including excerpts from 'Madrigalia', a new sequence which grew out of songs written for the composer Gavin Bryars. Nine of the poems here also appeared in *Pendle Witches*, illustrated by Paula Rego and published by Enitharmon in 1996.

Contents

III

IV

V

I

The Kiss

His Buick was too wide and didn't slow,
our wing-mirrors kissing in a Suffolk lane,
no sweat, not worth the exchange of addresses.

High from the rainchecking satellites
our island's like a gun set on a table,
still smoking, waiting to be loaded again.

On Sizewell Beach

There are four beach huts, numbered 13 to 16,
each with net curtains and a lock.
Who owns them, what happened to the first twelve,
whether there are plans for further building:
there's no one here today to help with such enquiries,
the café closed up for the winter,
no cars or buses in the PAY AND DISPLAY.
The offshore rig is like a titan's diving board.
I've heard the rumours that it's warmer here
for bathing than at any other point along the coast.
Who started them? The same joker who bought
the village pub and named it the Vulcan,
'God of fire and metalwork and hammers,
deformed and buffoonish, a forger of rich thrones'?
Whoever he is, whatever he was up to,
he'd be doused today, like these men out back,
shooting at clay pigeons, the rain in their Adnams beer.
And now a movement on the shingle
that's more than the scissoring of terns:
a fishing boat's landed, three men in yellow waders
guiding it shorewards over metal-ribbed slats
which they lay in front of it like offerings
while the winch in its hut, tense and oily,
hauls at the hook in the prow, the smack with its catch
itself become a catch, though when I lift
the children up to see the lockjaws of sole and whiting
there's nothing in there but oilskin and rope.

I love this place, its going on with life
in the shadow of the slab behind it,
which you almost forget, or might take for a giant's
    Lego set,
so neat are the pipes and the chain-mail fences,
the dinky railway track running off to Leiston,

4

the pylons like a line of cross-country skiers,
the cooling ponds and turbine halls and reactor control
   rooms
where they prove with geigers on Open Days
('Adults and Children over 14 years only')
that sealed uranium is less radioactive than a watch.

One rain-glossed Saturday in April
a lad from Halesworth having passed his test
and wanting to impress his girlfriend
came here in the Ford he'd borrowed from his father
and took the corner much too fast, too green to judge
the danger or simply not seeing the child
left on the pavement by the father – no less reckless –
who had crossed back to his Renault for the notebook
he'd stupidly forgotten, the one with jottings
for a poem about nuclear catastrophe,
a poem later abandoned, in place of which
he'd write of the shock of turning round
to find a car had come between him and his daughter,
an eternity of bodywork blotting out the view,
a cloud or an eclipse which hangs before the eyes
and darkens all behind them, clearing at last
to the joy of finding her still standing there,
the three of us spared that other life we dream of
where the worst has already happened
and we are made to dwell for ever on its shore.

Havens

Come to the window, sweet is the night air!

A brass bedstead, a record still turning,
a pair of empty tumblers in the sink:

while history filled its tanks outside the door
there were always such places to miss it for,

rooms with wine stains and a speckled mirror
unknown alike to the ball-turret gunner

and the captain with his blinding spurs.
If things got out of hand you shut the shutters.

Even the study, the cold spot of the house,
could be warmed and soundproofed by new verse.

Then what's this danger that passes through bricks?
How come we are melting away like this?

Flats

We kept ourselves to ourselves.
Like one-night tenants of a cheap motel,
we didn't bother with the others.
Faces passed. Names lay unclaimed
in the front door's cage of mail.

Just once, rising through the stairwell,
a woman's sexual cries – her throat in spate
transcending all partitions, as if to prove
how noisy and important love must be
that it alone got through.

Not quite: it features in my vision of hell.
They have cordoned off the world
into couples and couples, all separate,
all being made to listen to
some love that will never be theirs.

Fuel Debts Enquiry

When I surveyed the wondrous New Cross blocks,
layers of eyes froze behind spyholes.

'I can/cannot afford to heat my living-room':
interviewers circle as appropriate.

The flats massed like an iceberg, nine-tenths in the
    blue,
strung together by a lift I did not dare take.

Rung after rung I mounted, rang down corridors,
hung about for answers twenty floors up.

Inscrutable, screwed to the wood, threshold lenses
telescoped my well-meant profile.

Dogs barked, carpeted steps secretly came and went,
the Cyclops stare guarded all who dwelt in there.

I did/did not establish who was in arrears.
I could get some/no statistics on the coldness inside.

We Won't Get Fooled Again

Among the Saturday bargains – hose pipes,
open-crotch panties, inflatable chairs –
this one: 'Front-door spyhole. Six-foot span.
You see unwanted callers. They don't see you.'

The picture's inspired. A curlered housewife
safe behind her door figures immediately
the scar-faced stranger looming outside
is not selling brushes. She won't open up.

Europe's new frontier! The end of the terror!
Never again those games of happy families
cut short by a rap in the heart of the door –
father leaving us to answer it,
then the loud, unfamiliar voices
and the silence for a moment or two.

Flood

We live in the promise of miraculous lakes:
Dagenham, Greenwich, Wapping, the Isle of Dogs.

'When the siren sounds, those in the blue environs
should proceed immediately to non-risk zones.'

Spring tides, high winds: for days we can hear
of nothing else, our eyes bright with disaster,

our dreams a chronicle of *mountaing anarchie,
the river-folke frantick, shippës trappt in trees.*

*And the dove we sent out, when it came back,
had the brown glaze of estuaries on its beak.*

In our dreams no sandbags hold back the flood:
we would bring the whole world down if we could.

Theory of Heredity

The generations come down on you –
like football crowds when a goal is scored.

It began when a sperm, waving its scarf excitedly,
tick-ticked its way in through the turnstile.

Now it's reached hundreds – parents, and their parents,
and the ones before that, stacked on the terraces

as high as sight, and you're at the bottom.
And when their tassels heave like a harvest-field

you will heave along, though you thought
by now you could go which way you pleased.

Superstore

Sunday, late, at the superstore,
a fresh wind across the car park
plaining through the trolley's mesh,
and doors that slide apart
on a carnival of promo flags,
a vault of infinite shelves.

Baths, tiles, kiddyseats, barbecues,
woodfiller, Polyfilla, turps,
radios and alarm clocks
separate or in wedlock,
pinewood pews set under smoky tabletops,
rolls of insulation that bring us

round a corner to PRODUCE –
coley and fish fingers,
French loaves and granary loaves,
apples and potatoes laid out
as for Harvest Festival
beside a fan of dried-up flowers.

I could go on, and do go on,
past the fly-mos on a prickly strip
of astroturf, the wheel-less wheelbarrows,
the grass seed, weedkiller, lawn feed,
the gnomes fishing lucklessly
in the pre-mould of a pond.

And beyond to the fashion grove,
the aisles of dresses waiting there
like princesses for the awakening touch,
the coat-hangers like Cupid's bows
carried off to screened confessionals
where we try out new versions of ourselves.

But that's enough for now: we heave
the trolley to the log-jammed checkout
where girls with singing typewriters
record our losses onto spools
of print-out which they hand us
with an absent smile.

Then out onto the tarmac
past a car boot spilling over
with the corpses of cement bags
and a man and his wife shouting
at each other like Pyramus and Thisbe
through the vents in a louvre door.

And there's not much left of Sunday,
dusk lowering on the roof-racks,
another weekend gone into nothing
as the red-eyed tail-lights
file through the tollgate,
leaving behind the superstore,

its row of lights like the buttons
on a keyboard, its glowing crypts
not a mockery of churches
but a way like them of forgetting
the darkness where no one's serving
and there's nothing to choose from at all.

The Rack

Love wins out but look at all the corpses.
The hero's dais is made of broken bones.
The silence of the dead is not acceptance.
Hearts are dangling like vandalised phones.

The man applauding hasn't been told yet.
Troops are digging where the campion unfurled.
The bride slips her hand inside the bridegroom
as we stretch out on the rack of this tough world.

II

A Provincial Fiction

These fields are pale with the myth
of faithless sons gone south
to the 'airs and graces of the city'.

All's lost through the loss of them:
hands dwindle at the farm
and the woods are a sighing of chainsaws.

Doctor says there's little hope.
Will you be coming up?
We've kept your room just as it always was.

The stone fires, the piebald hide
of hillsides under broken cloud,
these grounds they had and will not go back on.

Metamorphoses of Childhood

I

With my pair of labradors I lay
like Romulus under the kitchen table.

We'll be back at six, my parents would say,
abandoning me to the wolf-toothed nanny.

High above me her hands were baking
on a floured, unreachable shelf.

Later came squabbles with my fat twin-sister:
I was the handier, it seemed,

and to prove it constructed in days
a bakelite replica of Burnley.

II

*The train runs right through the middle of the
   house . . .*
Well, almost: they were the giants in our hedge,

breathing fire from their sooty toppers,
the burdens of the world on their back.

They were fetching for magnates:
coal, cotton, shearings of quarry.

Cars queued up to hear them at the crossing.
Our teacups trembled on tenterhooks.

I pined for release from the attic room
where a slip of the tongue had confined me.

III

Misery had no bedtime: it fell
like lead in the middle of the night.

Boum, boum, boum, boum – it was the sound
Of boredom in my bloodstream,

the high room coming and going.
Why would the cornices never stay still?

First I was an elephant,
then a pin in the infinite spaces.

Marapa, marapa, I'd cry,
but my parents never heard me.

IV

Where there's muck, there's brass they said,
as in the coppery shine of cow-pats.

But then I discovered the salt-lick,
a blue whetstone lighting up the fields.

I'd been reading Scott Fitzgerald's
'The Diamond as Big as the Ritz'

and carried it home like a pools-win,
a sapphire from the mud. When I learnt the truth

it shrank in my grasp like an ice-pack:
I wept to be a prisoner of fact.

Death sauntered in adjoining rooms,
familiar and airy as linen.

It was the dent in Grandpa's chair,
his saying *night-night* and never returning.

Heaven must be nice: his coffin
looked plusher than a chocolate box.

And hell was just a nettle-sting
or scorch from fireworks – only ages to heal.

Why, then, Daddy's tear, lying like a lens
on my new pointy-black shoes?

Cuckoo-pint

A brown matchstick held up in the wind,
the bract-leaf cupped around it like a palm.

March had not extinguished it: there it lurked,
sly as something done behind the sheds,

slithering from its half-unrolled umbrella
as we snipped pussy-willow from the lanes.

To come instead on this old man of the woods,
tanned and cowled and clammed inside his collar,

his shirt-front splattered with tobacco stains,
his poker oozy with tuber-froth,

was like learning by accident a secret
intended for later, exciting

and obscene and not to be gone back on,
like the knowledge of atoms, or death.

Pomagne

'Be careful not to spill it when it pops.
He'd bloody crucify me if he caught us.'

We had taken months to get to this,
our first kiss a meeting of stalagmite

and stalactite. The slow drip of courtship:
her friend, June, interceding with letters,

the intimate struggle each Friday
under the Plaza's girder of light.

But here we were at last, drinking Pomagne
in her parents' double bed, Christmas Eve

and the last advent-calendar door.
'Did you hear the gate click?' 'No, did you?'

Pendle Witches

On recs and at swimming pools
we searched for the girl
– shy and uncomeatable –
through whose glimming thigh-tops

the light would make a perfect O,
that florin emptiness
not the token of a virgin
but the hole in a lemmel-stone

to ward off the hags
who ran the Pennines
and who wanted to trap us
in the sossy peat of their maw.

Whinny Moor

Old people will tell you that after death the soul passes over Whinny-moore, a place full of whins and brambles, and . . . would be met by an old man carrying a huge bundle of boots; and if among these could be found a pair which the bare-footed soul had given away during life, the old man gave them to the soul to protect its feet whilst crossing the thorny moor.

I was back walking on Lothersdale Moor,
through ling, blackthorn and blips of sheepshit,
over dry-stone walls and up kestrels' airstreams,
back with the becks and original sources,
to land on the fell road under Pinhaw
beside the steamed-up hatchback of a Ford.

The driver's window opened as I stood there.
'Tha'll catch thi death – get in an warm' thisen'
said the heathery face, open, bloodshot,
leaning across to unlock the other door.
I limped around and took my seat beside him,
cupping my bones about his leather flask.

That highland nip restored me to the land
of the living and I warmed to my tale:
how I had hiked the backs of the Pennine Way,
leaving at dawn from Todmorden to end –
'down there, see, if this mist would just clear up
a bit' – in the shade of Thornton Church.

He glanced, disbelieving, at my plimsolls,
frayed and holy with a flapping sole.
He was a rep for Peter Lord, he said,
nodding behind him at the bootful of boots.

'Ah've worked in shoes near alf a century
an sin all t'flippin lot go reet down'ill.'

Then he asked who I was. 'Morrison, eh,
a name for up ere. I knew thi father well
an t'ole surgery in Water Street.
E did is best by Earby, wi disease an that,
aye an thi mother too, deliverin bairns.
Ad thi no mind to follow in their shoes?

'Ere, ave another swig – tha's like a sheet
what started out as peachy then lost
its colourin in t'wash. Ah tell thi what:
you tek these pumps off me to elp thi ome.
They're seconds, any road, an just your size,
an tha's some sloggin still to Thornton.'

Then I was out beside him shaking hands
as he clattered off across a cattle grid,
turning left down to Elslack by the pines.
He should have come out by the Tempest
but the roak was too mawky to see beyond
the reservoir and he vanished in thin air.

That cardboard box was all I had to show
for our meeting, its pair of char-black pumps
like the ones I'd brought from school for Simon
     Holmes
the Christmas after his accident,
the lorry that flicked him from his bicycle
turning my mate into a sickbed ghost.

I laced the eyelets for the journey on
across the bogs and sandylands of moor.
Beside the ink-blot of a rookery
I could make out the nib of Thornton Church,

and up behind, like an act of kindness,
a perched, solitary, whitewashed farm.

And in the gorse and peat and heather-scorch
his voice came back again like judgement,
the voice of the tarns with their millstones,
a cairn of slingshot stopping me in my tracks
until the wind brought the grit of a Hargreaves
or one of the Barnoldswick MacSweens:

Get on wi thee, stuck there in t'eather
maunderin and moulderin like a corpse.
What odds would it ave made tha stayin put?
Didst think tha could cure us like thi father?
If tha'd not buggered off at twenty
tha'd as like be a boss at Silentnight,

layin us off wi no brass or future
in this valley of dead vases an mills.
So thank thi lucky stars yon ol divel's
gi'en thi some pumps to get ell out again
an shift thisen sharpish to t'nearest stickle
afore tha's eaten up by t'worms or us.

Back

A griming of snow along the moortops,
water-beads sissing across the Aga,
sunlight wading through a summer-colt,
the lawn slaphappy after a shower:

before I know it I've descended to this,
a stone rectory lording it in the Pennines,
ringed by horse-chestnuts and a rookery,
near the flush Leeds–Liverpool canal.

You can drop the accent but you never lose
the slang of memory – for belled foxdocks,
the swint-ways chittering of swallows,
the lovely dung-reek of Betty Metcalf's dress.

A long shiver down the back of the land:
even in June it has that chilliness,
wind stevening over the switchbacks,
the water-meadows ruffled then glossy

like the fur down a labrador's spine.
From a far city I keep that place on
for my dream-life, a home to home in on
when I'm asleep or at the brow of it,

heart racing like our drophead Triumph
when we took the canal bridge at West Marton,
its whitewalled tyres as we hit the humpback
treading air for a moment like young lambs.

III

Mates

They are holed up in some bar among the dives
of Deptford, deep in their cups and a packet
of cashew nuts, like Chippy Hackee and cute
little Timmy Tiptoes hiding from their wives.

Any minute now they'll be talking shop
about some crony's record-breaking bender,
like that mate of Terry's banned from his own do
after sinking twenty vodkas and a cop.

Set them up again: I'm holding my tankard
so the cloudy light will set them up –
this mermaid on a forearm, that chinstrap
of a scar – though I'll try not to look hard

for fear of finding myself there, out on the piss
with a black-eyed, sulphurous misogynist.

Him

Like an Arctic fox snapping up grounded guillemot
    chicks
he hangs out in the parks and wastegrounds, the id of
    cities,
for time to bring her to this pretty pass.

Something has broken from the front of his mind
leaving just the back of it, a daubed cave of hunters
    and hunted
where no one but these girls can be allowed.

So he waits for them, leggy like deer in their ankle
    socks,
loud with an innocence he takes for the lack of it,
full of themselves, full of their mums and dads.

This one especially, wet-eyed as a leveret:
at the corners of sight she flickers like a red ignition
    light,
coming and going in her striped neck-scarf and PVC
    mac.

And soon there'll be a day she peels off from the
    others –
a buckle to be fastened, a brooch to be gone back for –
and then will be the time to introduce himself.

She is the special one who'll grow up in his care,
if she would only stop that screaming, if she could only
be made to understand him, but this is the only way.

Working in lines like beaters at a grouse-shoot,
we go on searching, stony among ferns and bracken,
unable to spring her from his trap.

The Ballad of the Yorkshire Ripper

The 'Red Death' had long devastated the country. No
pestilence had ever been so fatal, or so hideous. Blood
was its Avatar and its seal . . .
  Edgar Allan Poe, 'The Masque of the Red Death'

I were just cleaning up streets our kid. Just cleaning
up streets.
  Peter Sutcliffe to his brother Carl: . . . *somebody's*
  husband, somebody's son . . . by Gordon Burn

> Ower t'ills o Bingley
> stormclouds clap an drain,
> like opened blood-black blisters
> leakin pus an pain.
>
> Ail teems down like stair-rods,
> an swells canals an becks,
> an fills up studmarked goalmouths,
> an bursts on mind like sex.
>
> Cos sex is like a stormclap,
> a swellin in thi cells,
> when lightnin arrers through thi
> an tha knows there in't owt else.
>
> Ah've felt it in misen, like,
> ikin ome part-fresh
> ower limestone outcrops
> like knuckles white through flesh:
>
> ow men clap down on women
> t'old em there for good
> an soak up all their softness
> an lounder em wi blood.

It's then I think on t'Ripper
an what e did an why,
an ow mi mates ate women,
an ow Pete med em die.

I love em for misen, like,
their skimmerin lips an eyes,
their ankles light as jinnyspins,
their seggy whisps an sighs,

their braided locks like catkins,
an t'curlies glashy black,
the peepin o their linnet tongues,
their way o cheekin back.

An ah look on em as kindred.
But mates all say they're not,
that men must have t'owerance
or world will go to rot.

Lad-loupin molls an gadabouts,
fellow-fond an sly,
flappy-skets an drabbletails
oo'll bleed a bloke bone-dry:

that's ow I ear em spoke of
when lads are on their tod,
an ow tha's got to leather em
to stop em gi'in t'nod.

An some o t'same in Bible
where Paul screams fit to bust
ow men are fallen creatures
but womenfolk are wust.

Now I reckon this fired Peter,
an men-talk were is goad,
an culprit were our belderin God
an is ancient, bullyin road.

No, Pete weren't drove by vengeance,
rountwistedness or ale,
but to show isen a baufy man –
but let me tell thi tale.

      *

Peter worked in a graveyard,
diggin bone an sod.
From t'grave of a Pole, Zapolski,
e eard – e reckoned – God,

sayin: 'Lad, tha's on a mission,
ah've picked thi out o t'ruck.
Go an rip up prostitutes.
They're nobbut worms an muck.

'Streets are runnin sewers.
Streets are open sores.
Get in there wi thi scalpel
an wipe away all t'oors.'

Pete were pumped like a primus.
E felt is cravin whet.
E started cruisin Chapeltown
but e didn't kill, not yet.

E took a job on t'lorries,
a Transcontinental Ford.
E felt reet good in t'cabin.
E felt like a bloody Lord.

E'd bin a bit of a mardy,
angin on t'old dear's skirt.
E didn't like folks shoutin,
or scraps wi lads, or dirt.

E'd watch his dad trough offal –
trotters, liver, tripe –
or pigeon scraped from t'by-pass,
or rabbit, ung an ripe,

an all e'd felt were babbyish,
a fustilugs, alf-nowt,
an wished e were is younger kid
tekkin lasses out.

But now e'd started truckin
an ropin up is load
an bought isen a Bullworker
e swelled up like a toad,

an stuck is ead in motors
an messed wi carbs an ubs,
an drove wi mates to Manningham
an other arse-end pubs,

or sometimes off to Blackpool
to t'Tower or lights or pier,
or waxworks Chamber of Orrors –
aye, Pete were allus theer.

E met a lass called Sonia,
a nervy type, a shrew,
oo mithered im an nattered,
but Pete, e thought she'd do.

She seemed a cut above im,
a teacher, arty too,
oo wanted summat more'n kids.
Aye, Pete, e thought she'd do.

Cos Sonia, she weren't mucky,
not like yon other bags,
them tarts in fishnet stockins,
them goers, buers, slags.

                *

Voice said 'Lad, get crackin:
ah've med thi bombardier.'
Pete blasted red-light districts,
eight lasses in two year.

E slit em up on wasteground,
in ginnel, plot an park,
in cemetery an woodyard,
an allus after dark.

Is tools were ball-pein ammers,
acksaws an carvin knives,
an a rusty Phillips screwdriver
oned for endin lives.

Cops dint fuss wi fust three,
paid to out on street,
though e blunted blade on is Stanley
deguttin em like meat.

Nor minded marks on fourth lass,
ripped up in her flat,
wi both ends on a clawammer,
split-splat, split-splat, split-splat.

But Jayne MacDonald were a shopgirl
sellin nobbut shoes.
Pete, e killed er anyway
an now e were front-page noos.

They appointed a Special Detective,
George Oldfield e were called.
E looked like a country bumpkin,
puffin, red, alf-bald.

E fixed up a Ripper Freefone,
Leeds 5050,
an asked Joe Soap to ring im up
an 'Tell us what you know.'

An folks, they give im names all right:
cousins, neighbours, mates,
blokes what they didn't tek to –
all were candidates.

But Pete, no e weren't rumbled.
E moved to a slap-up ouse,
pebbledash an wi a garden,
an utch to keep is mouse.

Cos Sonia, though she nittered
an med im giddyup,
were potterin too long in t'attic
to mind that owt were up.

An she went so ard at paintin
an scrubbin on ands an knee
she nivver noticed blood on trews
an t'missin cutlery.

*

Two weeks afore they'd folks roun
to drink to movin in
Pete ad topped another lass
an not a soul ad sin.

Now, after tekkin guests ome,
e went to t'mouldy corpse
an slashed it wi a glass pane
an serrated neck wi saws.

E were a one-man abattoir.
E cleavered girls in alves.
E shishkebab'd their pupils.
E bled em dry like calves.

Their napes as soft as foxglove,
the lovely finch-pink pout,
the feather-fern o t'eyelash –
e turned it all to nowt.

Seventh lass e totted
were in Garrads Timberyard.
E posted corpse in a pinestack
like Satan's visitin card.

Eighth were a badly woman
oo'd just come off o t'ward
o Manchester Royal Infirmary
an went back stiff as board.

E id is next on a wastetip
under a sofa's wings.
E stuffed her mouth wi ossair.
Er guts poked through like springs.

An wee Jo Whitaker, just 19,
an Alifax Buildin clerk,
bled from er smashed-egg foread
till t'gutter ran sump-dark.

There were lorry-oil inside er,
an filins in each pore,
which might ave led to Peter
if police ad looked some more.

But Oldfield, e weren't tryin.
E'd ears for nobbut 'Jack':
some oaxer wi a cassette tape
ad sent im reet off track.

Voice on tape were a Geordie's,
a tauntin, growlin loon:
'They nivver learn, George, do they.
Nice chattin. See you soon.'

George fell line an sinker,
a fishhook in is pride:
'E thinks e's cock o t'midden
but I'll see that Jack inside.'

Aye, George e took it personal,
a stand-up, man to man,
like a pair o stags wi horns locked
– but Ripper offed an ran,

an wi George left fightin boggarts
e struck again like bleach:
bang in t'middle o Bradford
e wiped out Barbara Leach.

Then Marguerite Walls in Farsley,
strangled wi a noose
(a change from t'usual colander job,
none o t'normal clues).

     *

Everyweer in Yorkshire
were a creepin fear an thrill.
At Elland Road fans chanted
'Ripper 12 Police Nil.'

Lasses took up karate,
judo an self-defence,
an jeered at lads in porn shops,
an scrawled stuff in pub Gents,

like: 'Ripper's not a psychopath
but every man in pants.
All you blokes would kill like him
given half a chance.

'Listen to your beer-talk –
"hammer", "poke" and "screw",
"bang" and "score" and "lay" us:
that's what the Ripper does too.'

Aye, e did it again one last time,
to a student, Jacqueline Hill,
in a busy road, wi streetlights,
in a way more twisted still,

blammin er wi is Phillips –
but rest o that ah'll leave,
out o respect to t'family
an cos it meks me eave.

Now cops stepped up on pressure.
George, e got is cards.
Files were took from is ands
an put in Scotland Yard's.

They talked to blokes on lorries
an called at Pete's ouse twice,
but Sonia allus elped im out
wi rock-ard alibis.

It were fluke what finally nabbed im.
E'd parked is car in t'gates
of a private drive in Sheffield
wi ripped-off numberplates.

Lass oo e'd got wi im
were known to work this patch.
Cops took em both to t'station
but adn't twigged yet, natch.

Ad e meant to kill er?
E'd brought an ammer an knife
but maundered on alf evenin
ow e cunt stand sight o t'wife.

Then lass passed im a rubber
an come on all coquettish.
But still e didn't touch er.
It were like a sort o death-wish.

E managed to ide is tackle
sayin e wanted a pee.
But later on is ammer
were found by a young PC.

So cops they lobbed im questions
through breakfast, dinner, tea,
till e said: 'All right, you've cracked it.
Ripper, aye, it's me.

'Ah did them thirteen killins.
Them girls live in mi brain,
mindin me o mi evil.
But ah'd do it all again.

'Streets are runnin sewers.
Streets are open sores.
Ah went there wi mi armoury
to wipe away all t'oors.

'Ah were carryin out God's mission.
Ah were followin is commands.
E pumped me like a primus.
Ah were putty in is ands.'

*

This were nub o t'court case:
were Peter reet or mad?
If lawyer could prove im a nutter
e'd not come off as bad.

Were e bats as a bizzum
or t'devil come from ell?
Choice were life in a mental
or a Parkhurst prison cell.

E sat in dock like a gipsy
wi is open sky-blue shirt
an gawped at judge an jury
as if all t'lot were dirt.

Defence called up their experts,
psychiatrists an such,
oo sed Pete weren't no sadist
an didn't rate sex much,

that e'd suffered paranoia,
allucinations too,
an killed cos is mind ad drove im –
so t'gravestone tale were true.

But t'other lot med mincemeat
o those who'd bin Pete's dupe
showin ow e'd outflanked em
to get isen from t'soup.

Cos why, if e were loopy,
ad e allus killed on t'dot,
Friday nights an Saturdays,
in cold blood not in ot?

An why, if e weren't no sadist,
ad e left girls, more 'n once,
wi a hundred stabs in t'breastbone
an planks shoved up their cunts?

An ad he shown repentance
for 't'lasses' or for 't'oors'?
As for t'religious mission:
e'd med it up, of course.

(All through this Pete's bearin
were cold as a marble slab,
ard as a joint from t'freezer,
slant as a Scarborough crab.)

Counsels rested cases.
Jury reasoned it through.
Judge said: 'How do you find him?'
'Guilty – ten to two.'

They oicked im off in a wagon
past lynchers urlin abuse
an placards urgin t'government
BRING BACK CAT AND NOOSE.

They took im to Parkhurst Prison
to serve is time an more,
an folks said t'other inmates
would know to settle t'score.

But when is face were taloned
wi a broken coffee jar
it weren't for rippin real flesh
but nudes from t'prison *Star*.

An meanwhile rest o t'Sutcliffes
spent up their Fleet Street brass,
an put the boot in Sonia:
'Job's all down to t'lass.

'Our Pete were nivver a nutter.
E'd allus a smile on t'face.
That Sonia nagged im rotten
till e killed oors in er place.

'Cos that's the rub wi women,
they push us blokes too far
till us can't be eld responsible
for bein what us are.'

*

So tha sees, nowt's really altered
though Peter's out o t'way.
Mi mates still booze an charnel.
Weather's same each day.

Ower t'ills up northways
stormclouds thump an drain
like opened blood-black blisters
leakin pus an pain.

An death is like a stormclap,
a frizzlin o thi cells,
a pitchfork through thi arteries,
an tha knows there in't owt else.

It meks me think on Peter,
an what e did an why,
an ow mi mates ate women,
an ow Pete med em die.

Ah love em for misen, like,
their skimmerin lips an eyes,
their ankles light as jinnyspins,
their seggy whisps an sighs,

tiny tarn o t'navel,
chinabowl o t'ead,
steppin cairns o t'backbone,
an all e left for dead.

An I look on em as kindred.
But mates all say they're not,
that men must ave t'owerance
or world will go to rot.

An Pete were nobbut a laikin
o this belderin, umped-up God,
an served is words an logic
to rivet girls to t'sod.

An I don't walk appily out no more
now lasses fear lads' tread,
an mi mates call me a Bessy,
an ah dream of all Pete's dead,

an ow they come again to me,
an we croodle out o eye
in nests o fern an floss-seave
an fillytails in t'sky,

an ah mend em all wi kindness
as we kittle out on t'fells
an learn us t'ease o human love
until there in't owt else.

Isabella's Song

'I do hate him – I am wretched – I have been a fool.
Beware of uttering one breath of this to anyone at
the Grange.'

Wuthering Heights

As I stepped out one summer night
to feed my white ring-dove
a shadow fell across the gate
and swore undying love.

The shadow stretched out tall and slim,
its face was black as night.
It spoke to me of wedding-rings
and bridesmaids bathed in light.

I left my ring-dove's pretty cote
and took that shadow's hand
and let it touch my petticoat
and ease my belly-band.

Its fingers felt as light as air.
It called me its sweet belle.
But when it lay on top of me
it crushed me like a shell.

Now I'm a shadow of myself.
I bear that shadow's bairn.
I'm running off down London way
to hide my body's shame.

So don't step out one summer night
and leave your white ring-dove.
A shadow fades as sunlight does.
Don't trust a shadow's love.

IV

Epithalamion

Cart-tracks, drove-roads,
coast-paths and bridle-ways,
lanes banked high with campion and rose:

along the dotted lines of England
we signed away one summer
mile after mile after mile.

Madrigalia

Just as the ash-glow
and cinderlight of the skies
lose all their lustre
once you've seen the moon rise,

and the volted daisies
and bruised delphiniums
pale into nothing
when the sunflower blooms,

and the swallows
plinking on their long string
sound merely garrulous
if you've heard the lapwing,

so the women I'd been eyeing
were a dimmed light
when you walked into vision
that first night.

*

I was living with someone.
Six months and going nowhere.
But he was kind to me.

Then you came, sending flowers,
writing, calling me at work,
battering my heart,

again and again
proposing drinks, dinner,
a play, a film, anything.

A walk by the river,
during lunch-hour,
was the most I'd grant.

You were all bellow
and nerve, like a heifer
in wide field-light.

To slow you down
I sat us on a river-bench
and made you talk

– talk to me, not gush.
Sun came off the oar-tips
of a passing boat-crew

and somewhere then
a ray went in and under
like a countermand

and I began to be yours.

      *

Within minutes, our first conversation,
I knew.
Out of nowhere, from the rim of a glass,
the flash
of knowledge, as if there were no choice.
Sewn up.
Like the moment the plane drops through
the clouds
and the land spreads out its patchwork,
and you see,
in crushing detail, the future race to meet you.
Just like that.

Please, love, don't go off so quickly.
Hang about. Get to know the place.
It's your heart I want planted inside.
When farmers have scattered their seed,
they stick around to help it grow.
Pass me some water, massage my thighs.
Wasn't it you five minutes back who
said you'd always be there for me
and promised – if I slept with you –
the earth? Surely the hero still has ammo
after firing one shot. What's your rush, then?
Stay a bit longer. Love me again.

*

Our bodies in the shower.
The hisp and plather
of skins under the water.
The smoke coming off us.
The stream within the stream.
We were rinsed clean
of everything but desire.

*

After bed, a shower.
After the shower, bed.
After round on round
of this, a bath
which I fell asleep in,
waking to find
my skin changed,
my toes and fingers,
which had been smooth
and flat before,
now contoured with

tors and hills,
the sort where
forts are pitched
for skirmishings.
Trouble, I thought,
not liking it at all.

*

The print of soles across the bathroom floor:
finding them, I felt like Crusoe, and stooped
to test their warmth and wetness, then rose
to follow where they led, not caring that
I knew the end already, as if she were
a stranger, this woman meeting my eyes
in the dressing-table mirror,
one towel tucked just above her bosom,
another knotted round her head,
and waterbeads still fresh on her nape
and shoulders, which I bent to kiss –
meeting your eyes again as I did –
for the first time ever in the world.

*

Your name in the phone book,
your voice on the answering machine,
your smiling photo in my purse
are steadier and more palpable than you
whose eyes when I look into them
fly off in different directions,
like woodpigeons startled out of a wood.

*

I should have seen from your eyes
and the lightning which broke in them
the storms that lay ahead.

The white ecstasy of bedsheets,
smashed pots and broken furniture,
the forked static of your touch.

But storms pass like headaches do.
Today the rain, in carpet-tacks.
Alone together, we watch the rain.

*

Ecstasy in August
the fish-leap of your muscles
honey under your tongue
and doves flying from your eyes.

There will be winter, too
but when I'm cold you'll fetch mulled wine for me
when I'm sick you'll feed me apples
when I'm sad you'll press lilies on my brow.

In April we'll fly to the Lebanon and live among the
    vines
and the vines will be young and tender
and our bed will smell of cinnamon
and I'll order them not to wake us till we please.

I'll keep you safe
If ever you're lost
I'll go about the streets and broadways
and find you and bring you to my bed.

And when I massage you with myrrh and lavender
your cock will be hard as ivory
and I'll make the rooks cry in your throat
as you come like a goat-kid in my face.

56

The milk will be balm to me
my skin like a sheepflock newly dipped and shorn
but with threads of scarlet where your nails have been
And you'll kiss every bloodline away.

My pomegranate in the wilderness
my sunlit fishpool
my August torrent
and winter coal.

No one can quench the flame
of this ecstasy
our love is strong as death
and rich as fire.

       *

We bought things for the flat to make it ours.
Correction: I did. You'd trek with me to stores
under duress and stand there while I chose
curtains or jugs or bits of furniture.
You'd even help carry them to the car.
But if I asked you what you thought,
'All right' was the most you'd ever say.
I put it down to your being male and tried
not to resent it or think the obvious,
that you didn't give a fuck about my choices
because you didn't give a fuck about us.

       *

She'd buy things, expecting our lives to flourish
because the objects surrounding them had changed.
My line was different: no matter how and where
we lived, we were what we were, unalterably.

       *

He'd come back late,
staying on at work
or out with friends.

I did the same
and tried not to notice
something had changed.

He was bored,
I saw that much,
seeing I was too.

But I said nothing
and nor did he,
as if to raise it

were disrespectful,
like unearthing a corpse,
our own as it turned out.

*

All the homely arts and crafts –
the soft plinth of a tongue,
the Guggenheim of an ear,
the weave of hands and hair –

are nothing next to the science
of these eyes unseen until tonight,
this lip lightly charred from
the soft combustion of a kiss.

*

Bags under his eyes,
tail between his legs
like an erratum slip,
he lands with his luggage

on the doorstep,
begging forgiveness
for his crime.

Behind me, on the desk,
an empty box of Kleenex
and a pen in the gutter
of my diary, where I've been
totting up his crimes:
'If the phone rang during sex,
he would stop to pick it up.'

So it's pity, nothing more,
opens the door for him,
allows the sorry-kisses,
lets him run me a bath
and fetch hot toddy:
this time I'm going
to give him what for.

*

The bed is empty.
The dark floods in.
I'm back at our place.
You're back with him.

A red-rimmed wineglass,
that brush of yours,
the sperm-sweet duvet
are all the spoors.

I'm someone else now,
a pseudonym.
The bed is empty.
You're back with him.

*

I went to an old lover, for sympathy.
But he came on like a quack doctor,
promising to cure me with his root.

Most men are like this:
no matter what wound we bear,
the same blunt stem's on offer.
And however good it feels
for half an hour, it never works.

Oh, for some gentler therapy –
flowers, a cuddle on the sofa,
a conversation with a man
who listens to me for once.

*

Who's the more to blame?
You for having eyes
a soul could drown in?
Or me for falling in?

Let's not argue who's to blame.
The only points at issue
are the ones that shrink
and widen in your eyes.

My eyes have grown dim
from patrolling the days
like a camera lens,
trawling for your eyes.

Here's you in New York.
Here's you in London.
Your eyes are everywhere.
Where are your eyes?

*

Nothing between us, or so it felt.
Skin, bone, saliva, sweat and breath –
which was you and which was me we couldn't say.

Nothing between us, or so it feels.
In bed turning away from each other,
and the valley filling up with snow.

*

We sat in the fork of an almond tree
as March came slowly into leaf.
Our love blossomed like a snow-storm.
White confetti paved the street.

What are we to do now autumn's here?
Your eyes are cold, my arms have shrunk.
The years seem a tangle of dry twigs.
Can we get through them without love?

A Child in Winter

Where is the man who does not feel his heart
softened . . . [by] these so helpless and so perfectly
innocent little creatures?

Cobbett

When the trees have given up,
snowberries come into their own,
winter grapes, albino
settlers of the dark.

With their milky blobs
they lined our doorstep
that November dusk
we swung your basket

up the gravel-path
and home. Child-Moses,
prince of the changing-mat,
heir of furry ducklings,

your babygros in drifts
on the clothes-rack,
we anoint your body's
rashes and folds.

When you cry it's like
some part of ourselves
breaking off and filling
these rooms with its pain.

Your breath's a matchflame
certain to go out,
we're at the cot hourly
holding our own.

In the shush of night-time
snowflakes crowd the window
like our own pale faces,
a shedding of old skins,

a blown seedhead,
paper pellets thrown down
by the gods to mark
your fiftieth day.

Lorries flounder on the hill.
We're out there watching
with a babysling
while the world goes under wool.

Little one, limpet,
resented stranger,
who has no time for me
and does not know time,

your home's the cradle
of a snowy hillfort
with pink turrets
and underground springs.

Daylight bores you: all night
you otter in our bed until
we wake to find you with us,
hands folded like a saint

accepting his death.
If it's we who must die first
that seems less costly now,
having you here like wheat.

Spring comes, measured
in light and celandines,
and your first tooth, faint
as a rock at low tide,

headstone for these trials
with cottonbuds and nappies,
your silver lips tracking
for comfort in the dark.

Sleep On It

Wrecked by our children
we sit among the spars
of a Chinese take-away,
washed up and hollow-eyed,
hanging on for nothing
but the Epilogue,
two ruined late-late lives.

Another night ahead
of waking from sleep's seabed
to the cry of a kittiwake,
a *waaa-waaa* dragging me
blind towards the child
among wave-tossed bedsheets
howling to be airlifted free.

The compulsion of people
to remake themselves
could die in a room like this,
a graveyard of ambition
where hopes lie scattered
with the Lego, a city
just abandoned or sacked . . .

But we'll be right again
by morning as light or love
haloes every game they play –
him grounded with his balsa
plane, she all at sea
in her puddle which glimmers
like a dropped silk dress.

Meningococcus

'My son has gone under the hill.
We called him after a clockmaker
but God meets all such whimsy
with his early-striking hands.

That night of his high fever
I held a stream against me,
his heart panicky as a netted bird,
globes of solder on his brow.

Then he was lost in sea-fret,
the other side of silence,
his eyes milky as snowberries
and his fifteen months unlearned.

They have taken him away
who was just coming to me,
his spine like the curve
of an avocet's bill.'

Kindertotenlieder

after Rückert and Mahler

I

So the sun intends to rise as usual
as if the world hadn't ended last night.

But it was only my world, and the sun still has work
to do, raising the living with its light.

Try to get out, they say. Don't hug the shadows.
As if what died was just a rose

and the heart could rise above it like the sun –
look! – razing the hills with its vast fire.

II

Now I get the point
of the dark burn of your pupils
as if you meant to concentrate
all you had and were
in a single, unforgettable stare.

'We'd have liked to stay,' they go,
'but weren't allowed. Look hard
before we're light-years from you.
These eyes you're gazing into now
will tonight be far-off stars.'

III

When your mother
comes into the room

and I turn to look
it's not her face I see
but your infectious smile
which used to play
like a redstart round
her skirts and hips
till in a seed-gust
you were gone.

And when she turns
the light on in the hall
it's as if you're there
beside her in the blaze,
my flesh and blood,
so palpable, we thought,
but just a trick of light
across the boards,
flitting in then out
before we knew.

IV

I often think: they're out walking, that's all.
Any minute they'll be back.
It's a lovely day. Relax.
Listen hard and you'll hear their cries.

Pipe down. They're out walking.
And if they've wandered
further than usual, up the hill,
we'll soon catch up with them.

They've run ahead, that's all.
When the sun's out on the hill,

we can catch up with them.
Listen hard and you'll hear their cries.

It's a lovely day, up on the hill.

v

I'd never have let them out in wind and rain like this.
I was not consulted when they went.
No one thought to warn me what I'd feel.

I'd never have let them out in wind and rain,
in case they caught a chill or worse.
No worse is going to happen now.

I'd never have let them out.
But the matter was taken from my hands.
They were only my children, see.

At least they're senseless now.
When lightning splits the sky,
and thunder breaks over their heads,
they lie immune,
at peace in the storm's dark eye,
at rest in their mother's home.

Somebody Loves Us All

I was tired, I suppose, and then hit ice,
no means of steering with the steering wheel,
the car sheering off into the crash rail,
the children waking with synchronised cries –

which is why we are here, in the lit hen-hut
of Motorway Recoveries, Snodland,
where an ESSO-hearted garage-hand
presses through the carbon of our invoice, not

rude exactly but unable to share
the drama of this happening to us,
the wall behind him trophied with photos
of his breakdown truck posed by the remainder

of Maestros and Escorts from which no one
could have passed on to this breathing-space
or heard their name read out into the mouthpiece
of a fingermarked, oil-anointed phone.

Ice Age

The heat's on full and our baby's flesh
is pargeted with eczema – flaky whorls
and roseheads, gone over with the oils
lined up here like magi round the crèche.

Fog, ice, Armageddon on the radio.
We can see from the nursery the ghost
of a lorry backed up in its exhaust,
like a polar bear fading into snow.

The trains have stopped running and the drainpipes
    too –
dried tears everywhere, the Night of the Long Knives,
a set of giant molars in the eaves.

Tusk, tusk, don't cry, mammoth will take care of you:
like stretched accordions the radiators hiss
their nonsense tunes, sealing us with a kiss.

Straw-burning

Was it *thrup* or *thrip*,
your word for the thunderflies
that came off the cornfield
with the paddlesteaming combine,
like wafted ashes

clagging to our bodies
and warning us of this:
the yellowing page
set alight at one corner,
the burning of straw?

We can see the flames
rushing towards us
like a lynch-mob,
blood in their eye,
tarring and furring,

until the churn and swirl
of the ploughed field-edge
brings them up short
as a river would
yards from our door.

But deaths come bittily
on the evening wind,
mouse bones and finch skulls,
burnt moths and butterflies,
a wedding from hell.

We take them to bed with us:
our charred dreams
are of a leak at Sizewell

or a Green Giant
razing villages and crops.

This morning they're inside,
these wisps of corn-soot,
making themselves at home,
feathering every windowsill,
shaken out of rugs

like rooks from a rookery
or depositing their tea-leaves
in our mugs.
And the mile-long fires
hanging their sheets

across the by-pass
are our summer's cremation,
the last of August
like a loose-leaf notebook
scattered round the globe.

Pick Your Own

Love among the loganberries,
the womby pods
and dangly genitalia
drawing us down the grass
with cartons and colanders,
baskets and cake-tins,
to the canes in rows
stiffened by fencing wire,
their bright notes
pitched against leaves
as sharp as steak-knives
and mean palisades of thorn.

Blackberries, blueberries,
whiskery gooseberries,
raspberries, tayberries,
florets of calabrese,
pippins, plum-bums,
rush-matted sweetcorn,
broad beans in ermine,
swan-necked courgettes,
straw-bedded strawberries,
squashed-on-the-floor berries,
beans pegged out like washing,
bottom-heavy pears:

here we go
down the lush corridors
of the PYO farm,
plucking and plundering,
pulling out the stops,
as an east wind
smelling of rape
rustles over lakes

of lapping polythene,
our children in warpaint
with giveaway stains
round their mouths.

And these long aisles
we walk for a season
are what freedom is,
or privilege,
under our own steam
driving here,
under our own yoke
bending to harvest,
the gates open,
the crops unguarded,
the earth not cracked by drought
or red with blood.

In the dead months
I open the freezer
and take from its clouds
a bag of bilberries,
holding it at my brow
like a compress,
shaking off the crystals,
undoing the tie,
then spilling out the gems
to weigh for dinner,
the fruits of history
tipping the scales.

Our Domestic Graces

The Chancellor of Gifts is an élitist.
You can't pretend he'll step out of the night
with a gilt invitation-card or flowers.
The brilliant words we wrote down in a dream
aren't there beside our bedside after all.

Yet something calls from the great expanse
of air we have made our latest home in.
Studio voices wake us near eight
with stories of God and how 'He moves among us
constantly like light'. What are his tracks like?

Mystery starts no further away
than these mossy footprints crossing the lawn
to where the raspberries are ripe again
and the panes of the greenhouse brim with tears.
Today even our lost city appears

from its shroud: a white dust-sheet slowly lifts
and here are all our glinting heirlooms –
the gasworks, like a coronet, queens it
over the houses, and bridges grace
the river with their lacy hems and Vs.

To have it all so clear – the congregating
chimneypots, the lines of traffic passing
over the heath like words being typed on a page.
Christ's fishermen must have felt like this,
crying out, amazed, at their spangled catch.

Light falls about these rooms, silvering the face
of what we are most used to, and ourselves,
who on such days might think we had been
elected at last – guest musicians
at the garden party of the gods.

Mist

Remember that old trick Mother used to play
on us at Christmas, how she would swathe
in layers of newspaper the necklaces
or bracelet charms she'd bought for us, then sink them
in a box inside another box, etc.,
so from thinking she'd given us a dolls' house
we'd be scrabbling through the skins of an onion
unable to find anything at all?

Well, I woke like that today, shawled in the fog
that had draped its fur about the cottage,
buried like a stone inside the tissue
of a jewellery box, a hair in the mohair
of a white Persian, awed but harboured
by petticoats and corset-ribs and underfrills,
as if the goddess of air had let down her skirts
to keep me from the monsters of the earth.

The clock said 7:10. Rising in a daze
I threw a duffel over my nightdress
and plunged through the porch's milky way –
then passed into new clouds of unknowing,
the book I'd stuck my nose in pressing me flat
between its endpapers, fazing and blitzing
till I felt like a finger in the Bible
searching for some marked didactic text.

Through the garden's smoky compartment
I picked my way outward to the road,
where cars drove from the screen they were showing
    on,
their eyes projectors picking out the spoolmarks
of cats' eyes, their beams roofbeams to crawl along
as they edged through the loft-space, arms held stiffly

to keep them from damage or extinction
under the lowered ceiling, the sunk roof of the world.

Struggling to breathe in all that breathiness,
I retreated to the balmy Aga
and waited for the fog to shuffle off.
But still the powers-that-be would not let be:
stalled drizzle caught in the fuzz of fir trees,
muswebs hung like tents in all the hedges,
and the sky loomed heavy as a wardrobe,
cloudbanks on its swirling walnut door.

Until the sun came down at last round lunchtime,
flaunting its flesh-blaze through négligé,
and I ate by the grille of a window
to witness the garden coming clean.
Only the field beyond would not confess itself,
the shy farmhand walking without legs
to where his tractor stood ticking in cling film,
the look of it more distant than the noise.

Layer by layer the mist peeled backward, a tide
retreating till the cottages and trees
that had been sunk beneath it drew up
to their full height. The grass breathed like a steam-
     bath,
herbed with rosemary and lavender,
drawing me out with a book and deckchair
for a pot of Lapsang on the lawn.
I must have nodded off very quickly,

the light behind my eyelids turning sour:
a huge dust-cloud blowing over the rye
was not just carrying dust. Out in the sticks
children's brains curdled in a blizzard of exhaust
     fumes.

79

The vapour in the woods changed from fox-breath
and spider-thatch to an acid stripping the pines.
And there were we in the thick of it,
out for a picnic in Rendlesham Woods,

Mummy pouring tea from a thermos
while Daddy took his penknife from the knapsack
to slice apart a gleaming hard-boiled egg.
A single egg, as you and I had been,
but now exploding into hemispheres –
Daddy dead, you gone west, me left behind
with Mother, who cried from her barkweave bedspread
to put her from this agony or else.

But when I woke in the morphine of evening
the sky was ridged with quiet like a scallop shell
and a thousand skitterish hedge-sparrows
were flocking in the newly turned-up field.
Sunset through their wings like aluminium,
they sheared off in plinkety fragments
or panicked together like a flapping sail
and swished in one blanket overhead.

Gauzed in muslin, the sun disappeared
way above the place it had been booked for,
soft-landing in rolls of insulation,
and in the dusk the fog crept back again,
stroking my thighs with its erotic tide,
courting me with white delphiniums,
like the night they couldn't get back from London
and left us for the first time by ourselves:

scared and excited we drank Tio Pepe
and pigged a double-decker Milk Tray,
and after, in the sweetpapers that clung
like smoky barnacles to the shagpile,

we played out our drama of abandonment,
Gretel and Gretel hugging each other tight
against the fear we felt, or said we did,
orphans of a pea soup, impossible to part.

How hard from where I am to explain it,
the difference from each other and that night!
Heatwaves and snow come and go like migrants.
Only mist shows that there is always mist,
how even when skies are scorched and see-through
still there's a point beyond the point you've got to,
washy, unfixable, a dead patch on the skin.
It's like starting going to church again,

the heavens boiling unattended
but their powdered air promising me the earth
is just our footstool, that there in the white-lying
fogbanks we shall find the missing lane.
And what we step into, though knowable,
is how we'd always failed to know it,
the air sweet, the brickwork soft against the cheek,
more light from the window than went into it –

or the common with white railings after rain
as two girls with a mud-red retriever
head off from the boredom of the touchline
and re-enter the drive to an estate,
a lion on each gatepost, the sun filtering through
fine as an auriscope, an arcade of limes
opening like a keyhole of eternity
on the grass-seamed cart track to the house.

Gisburne Park

'Originally dating from 1724, this former country home of
the Lords Ribblesdale opened as a hospital in 1985. Its loca-
tion overlooking acres of wooded parkland means that the
finest standards of care are complemented by the restful attrac-
tions of a rural environment.'

The thin-ribbed pillars in the entrance-hall
are the ones you came through for the Hunt Ball.

Beyond Reception and the waiting wheelchairs
was where you drank champagne by marble sculptures

or at the long white table helped yourself
to salmon, Aylesbury duckling or roast beef.

The talk was horsey: point-to-point, livery,
who was riding who. You shut up and ate the purée,

knowing, after port and coffee, you'd pass out
into the floodlit garden, to waltz and foxtrot

where a band played in the sagging, striped marquee.
Today there's just a lawn, six hoops in it for croquet,

rusting now, as if the spirit had slipped through
them of the place and the era – and of you.

But the floor upstairs, where you queued in Fifties
    dresses
for the Ladies, is crowded still, with nurses

at their stations to direct me to the room
where you lie, worn and nametagged, like a pilgrim

at journey's end. I hold your hand as I held it
then, seeing you dressed and powdered to go out,

a child, beside myself, unable to stop, again
and again pleading for you to stay – and again,

now, despite myself, by your bed, pleading the same.

Gone

You were always so slow to take your leave,
crumbs and tobacco dripping from your clothes
as you wheezed up from the depths of an armchair
like the sea-spilling, barnacled *Mary Rose*.

Cumuli of pipe-smoke would fill the porch
as you made heavy weather of your wellingtons
or fished in every pocket for a neckscarf,
fingering your toggles like precious stones.

And still the time to reach in that great chest
of yours for a word about the chances
of rain tonight, or to stand like a pillar
by the lawn-edge inhaling the crysanths.

Salt of the earth, monument to monuments,
who never hurried anywhere, except this once.

V

A Concise Definition of Answers

The city calls with its arches and spires
while the flatlands flourish with incest.
There are more curious things I wanted,
if possible, to touch on today –
how the sky, for instance, on these sultry afternoons
seems to settle round your forehead,

or the link between nostalgia and smell.
At this point science comes in, as you might expect,
or as you might yourself come in with that
colander of raspberries and rain. It seems like
everything we hoped for, as if the mayor had cut the
    tape
and events might finally begin.

But look, there's a storm blowing up, the sky
flickering like an old TV and the volume
almost deafening. Answers: I was holding them here
just now but they are gone again into those
cloud-lit days where martins and swifts sweep low
over the ground but can turn up nothing.

Grange Boy

Horse-chestnuts thudded to the lawn each autumn.
Their spiked husks were like medieval clubs,
porcupines, unexploded mines. But if
you waited long enough they gave themselves up –
brown pups, a cow opening its sad eye,
the shine of the dining-room table.

We were famous for horse-chestnuts. Boys
from the milltown would ring at our door asking
could they gather conkers and I'd to tell them
Only from the ground – no stick-throwing.
I watched from the casement as they wandered
in shadow, trousers crammed like mint-jars.

One morning they began without asking.
Plain as pikestaffs, their hurled sticks filleted
whole branches, the air filled like a pillowfight
with rebellion and leaves. I was alone.
I had not Father's booming voice. They were free
to trample through our peaceable estate.

Afterwards, matching Father in a show
of indignation (*bloody vandals and thugs*),
I imagined their home ground: the flagged backyards,
the forbidden ginnels and passages
winding up and out on purple moor,
the coal-sacks glistening in locked sheds.

It is June now, the chestnut scattered
like confetti. He summoned me today
to the billiard-room – that incident
with an apprentice. *I've told you before.*
A son in your father's firm, you're looked to
for an example. I don't know what to do.

So I sit at my rosewood desk, lines fading
across the parkland. I've been getting pamphlets
in a plain brown envelope and feel like
a traitor. Strangers have been seen
by the wicket-gate. Mother keeps to her bed.
English, we hoard our secrets to the end.

The Renunciation

Our lives were wasted but we never knew.
There was such work to be done: the watch-chains
and factories, the papers to sign
in the study. Surrounded by brass
how could we see what we amounted to –
a glint of eyes as headlights swept away?

In a cot on the lawn lies my nephew,
whose name I can't remember – the strands
of family thinner each year, though we
are here again, politely. The sun comes through
like a faint reminder of things not done:
forgotten dates, brothers not loved enough.

Peter, Jenny's husband, never forgave her.
When he caught them, out by the links, it was
all quite tame – some shouts and blows, Jenny
in tears, and the lover not showing again.
But later – well, Pete really cracked. Jen said he used
the affair as a way of opting out of things for good.

Here, on this stone, a relief map of lichen,
each mossy headland like a lush green future.
Swallows gather on the wire, darkening
the air with their forked legends – journeys
we planned to take too, had the time been right
and the distance to the airport less far

Every verse is a last verse, concluding
sadness. You hear its tone in the chestnuts
and rookery – how much has been taken.
The garden with its nightshade nags like some
vague guilt and the rooms look so untidy,
but there is nothing we know of to be done.

Simon has a sperm count of ten million –
almost no chance at all, the clinic said.
'Funny those years of worrying if the girl . . .
when all the time . . . And now Louise, who'd set
her heart on three at least . . . there's fostering, true,
  but. . .
I've lost the urge as well – know what I mean.'

I have learnt lately to admire the traits
of those who dispossess me: their scars,
their way of getting straight to the point,
things mattering. Their families roam the orchards,
at home among the tennis courts and lupins.
I watch – I have resigned myself to light.

Our lives run down like lawns to a sundial
and unborn children play in a world I imagine
as good: the sash cords run free again
and I am leaning out and calling them
to hurry now and join us quickly, will they,
quickly – we are all ready to begin.

Pine

Growing up under the weight of wardrobes,
we have awarded ourselves pine. The old veneers
have been stripped away. A Swedish wife welcomes us
with her frank stare and enlightened ideas.

White wood, bright wood, your blond shavings
fall away like the curls of a pampered child.
My fingers drift across the grainy fingerprints,
the dusty contours, the tumuli and cliffs.

Only these knots hold me, like some feud
from the past – the bad migraines my Mother
used to get, or a trough of low pressure
swishing its cloudbursts on the childhood fête.

But we will chamfer all that. When you called
this morning I was clearing our old dresser
of its tea-rings and nicks, the yellow sawdust
heaping up like salt-sift in a glass.

It's a walk through sand-dunes down to the sea,
the space where honesty might begin,
if we knew how, no corners to hide in,
the coming clean of our loyalties, and lies.

Xerox

They come each evening like virgins to a well:
the girls queuing for the Xerox machine,
braceleted and earmarked, shapely as pitchers
in their stretch Levi's or wraparound shirts,
sylphs from the typing pool bearing the forms
of their masters, the chilly boardroom gods.

But this one, this nervous one, is different.
She doesn't gossip with the others and pleads,
when it's her turn, *no, you go first*.
Not until they've gone, their anklets chinking
down the corridor, does she lift the hatch
and dip her trembling hand into the well.

A lightshow begins under the trapdoor:
it flashes and roars, flashes and plashes,
each page the flare of a sabotaged refinery
or the fission of an August storm.
Minutes pass, they slide into the wastebin,
but something is committed for all time.

Sweet-faced, two-faced, a face for every paper,
you were never so alone again.
They took a week or more to find you,
but they found you, posseed to the courtroom
under a scarlet rug, cheeks lit palely
in the lightning of a Nikon swarm.

And what has this to do with it? How you stood
one night by a heifers' drinking-trough
near Yelverton, afraid and down-at-heel
in a mud-churned, midge-drizzling negative,
then saw the country rising from its shadow
under the sudden candour of a moon.

The Inquisitor

I THE TASK

What trust would be like they never explained.
The eye of a deer miles away in woodland,
children running at the edge of a town . . .
But this was not their way of talking.
In a panelled room in an annexe
to the ministry they laid down all the terms.
Knowledge is death. Trust no one, least of all
friends. Loyalty? There are some secrets here
so terrible we keep them from ourselves.

So they gave you Finland, which was OK
at first but then it got boring. Contacts were scarce
– they had tightened the borders and the Gulf –
one sad Estonian, straight from Le Carré,
who shared with you ham omelettes, beer and *frites*.
You worked from home, mostly, the cottage
by the kalefields. Rachel, you were sure,
was having her first affair and you'd return
from Helsinki unannounced, hoping to surprise her.

There were times it felt like someone's dream
your own had got snared up with – the lies
to be told *for the sake of the country*,
the endless undertones like schoolboys
whispering in class. The weeks billowed
around you like a huge tent, roomy with light.
You leant back in the captain's chair
and got no further. The cases proved
intractable or turned out not to count.

Then came the call from the Director.
You do not smoke but watch him tapping

his cigarette against the silver case.
Your wife, yes, and children? He gazes down
to where the Thames and its bridges glitter
like a cold-frame. *A special job's come up.*
Someone arrived in London yesterday
we think may be of use. Be careful, now:
only scholarship will help you to survive.

But you must wait, you have been told you must,
and the paper they give you is just bumf.
The officials at their desks, light through
a venetian blind lining them like notepads,
Are engaged in lies. The text is for the enemy
while you proceed with oral tradition
in the outposts of the nation – a racecourse,
perhaps, or unpatronised bar, will bring
the muttered codeword from a stranger.

And the men, when they speak, are not reassuring:
scrabbling clerks, Pegasus bikeboys, stoolies
and sneaks, princes of the cubbyhole
and keyhole, neighbours charged with an exquisite
sense of duty, whose trade is the tip-off
and the unsigned note, who want no part
and don't appear in the acknowledgements page,
from whose sleek antennae nothing escapes,
the anonymous company of God –

and whose anonymous company you keep.
Today's one, trilby worn low as an eyeshade,
his collar's V deep as a railway cutting,
turned from the river to proffer two names:
Treslowa, Binjon. But where are these to take you?
Ironic light seemed to play about his eyes.
Even the reeds might seem to whisper

the betrayal of a king. There is nothing
in the river but reflection and waste.

II THE PRICE

The Senior Tutor has lent you his typescript
on 'Masculine Imagery in Donne'.
It would embarrass you to say so
but it lacks somehow the brilliance
of his conversation. Tact, then – silence is best.
The college garden blossoms with tongues.
End-of-term dances, tennis at midnight,
the summer solstice – you know even now
it can't go on like this, there's a price to pay.

She was just twenty-one, nice enough.
Left to itself it might have lasted six months.
But now this third ghosted beside you,
wrapped in a lucid mantle, crouched, hooded,
you cannot tell yet whether man or woman
(you dare not think whether yours or another's),
only that morning in the oasthouse
laying to rest the panic and reproaches:
By now even the fingernails are formed.

So this was love, like Lady's Slipper seeding
despite itself, a podburst of confetti
settling on the mourners by the churchyard gate.
You hardly know her but her body's changed
already, her nipples darkening to blue.
You bask in the cool of the canal-bank.
You inhale the breath of freezer-shelves.
You spread guide-books on a table, where by the end
of August your Europe is covered in dust.

Straightening and re-shaping a paperclip,
the Senior Tutor sounds faintly appalled.
He's kept his windows tight all summer.
Donne has been revised: *I make this link between
the hurrying-on of the comma'd line-ends
and the seducer's haste – it's going to rattle
all the Griersonites.* Coaxing the blind half-down
he keeps his back to you: *No luck, I'm afraid,
with your fellowship, but something else . . .*

That winter McAlpine cranes laboured and spun.
High above the classroom men in yellow helmets
strutted round like Hannibal on the Alps.
You were fitting children for offices,
their heads bowed, their biros toeing the line,
Something to tide you over. Rachel's mind
seemed to have gone completely. She moved about
like some long-legged seabird, plumaged with
the babythings she'd smother at her breast.

The child came early and was delicate.
He lay under his cloche like a frail plant,
seemed certain to die. Those nights in the hothouse
you cannot think straight or be sure of anything
but this ward of animal terror,
the authentic image of the world . . .
Until your son comes home at last, wall-eyed,
his silky skull throbbing like a hamster's,
a stranger and intruder, whom you love.

The ghosts of the smoky staffroom affect
to be delighted by the news. They mistrust
your appointment. They've observed you observing.
That trick of saying nothing when the knives
are out at tea-break has brought you both fear
and prestige. You're friends with three women

who feel like stones at the tidemark – cold, hard,
but with that silkiness underneath.
And with Maclelland, guerrilla of the text:

The horses in this poem, with their manes
of iron, symbolise a challenge to the state.
Their 'dinned hooves' are the drums of revolution.
They have thrown their jockeying leaders.
They are like gods hiding in the outfields
of the system, the beautiful ones
Who will return to set the ghostly cities right.
'Whinnying with rage', as the poet puts it,
they feel the power within them to stampede.

Harmless, no doubt, but Fitzroy loves it,
glubbing a Highland whisky in your glass.
Donne? He's had no time for Donne of late,
what with reviewing fiction for the *TLS*
and re-reading the Russian classics
(*A stick to beat the new boys with. Have you read*
John Fowles? I can't believe he's any good).
It's all there in his drawer of index-cards,
the names of the infamous on its tongue.

Another drink? Yes, you will need another
before disclosing any more. Come, come,
you must not think of this as treachery:
they are children playing near the flames
of history who need protection from themselves.
The names are unimportant, a matter
Just for us and these four walls. And in exchange
the formal letter, dropping like destiny
into the stained-glass puddle of your hall.

If this were art you might despise yourself
and confide to notebooks a squalid poetry

of excuse. But this is verse without the end-stops.
Last night was your entrée to the meeting-house:
Trots, feminists, fugitive professors,
ex-cobblers, martyrologists and Beats,
They welcomed you with Maclelland and spoke
of the attempt on the Observatory
and the Conrad assignation next week.

And Rachel and Ben? You'll do your best
To keep them out of this. Today, from your desk,
you see her climbing the hill with him,
a plastic carrier-bag lumpy with
new vegetables wedged inside the pushchair.
They move so painfully, with his hanging back
to gather stones and grass-blades, you've to step
out of the lamplight and hurry down
to meet them, your family, the one clean thing.

III TOPPING

There is a murder, as there has to be . . .
Scarpe grosse, cervello fino – his stealth
was learnt in the hills of Valtellina.
He kept his head down and his books clean.
He took the long train to the Russian front,
served with diligence, ate his mount in the snows,
and developed a taste for iced vodka.
Then he returned to make his fortune
in the banking cathedrals of Milan.

'When two people know a secret it is
a secret no more' – this was his motto,
and he was good at drawing secrets out
of others while not giving away his own.
He makes a pact with the Vatican
but learns his trade from the *sottobosco*,

the heirs of Garibaldi, who swear him in
on the back seat of a Mercedes
with the ritual of the masonic sword.

He rises to be Baron of the Treetops
and can see the gilt Madonnina
as he swivels his rosary-studded chair.
His office is vast and triangular,
with bullet-proof windows, a private lift
and eight gorillas posted at the door.
They say he sends aid to Solidarity.
On his antique desk he keeps a bottle
of mineral water, nothing more.

Dietro ci sono le tonache –
The cassocks are backing him to the hilt.
A shiny nameplate and a telex machine
have spread the word to the Bahamas.
It keeps on spreading – Luxembourg, Zurich,
Panama, Antwerp, Liechtenstein, New York.
He has nothing to give beyond a promise
but the next life is always about to happen
and the faithful buy enormous shares.

Until the police come like sceptics to dispute
in detail his Calvinist heresies and shams.
The Vatican stops its letters of comfort.
The organ-grinder flees, leaving only his monkeys.
Bruciato – ruined in an hour,
he descends to the dumb-show of the trading-ring,
The mania of tick-tack men, and knows he is done.
He moves with a lucid desperation
like his hurt secretary falling through air.

Assegno delle sette – the dawn arrest,
and the release on bail. He goes in retreat

to his converted barn at Drezzo,
feeding documents to the wood-burner,
and consoling himself with the works of Poe.
His two *marremani* sheepdogs howl like babies
as the nightwind infiltrates the door.
He eats a plate of cold chicken, then goes –
Klagenfurt, Innsbruck, Lake Constance, Gatwick,

to the divan in Chelsea Cloisters
where the *Loggia di Londra* will help.
But time is in the night like a hunter.
He shaves his moustache of a lifetime.
He turns the lock of his overnight bag
to its open sesame – o-o-o-o.
He takes his last effects – a black finger-glove,
a passport in the name Calvino,
and a cellophaned bank-wad of francs.

He stands above the unfamiliar streetlights
and waits for the door to knock, a friend's knock,
though a friend with needles and a motor-launch,
the act timed to perfection on the high tide –
for there has to be a murder, or suicide –
ten pounds of masonry in his turn-ups,
the nylon rope with two half-hitches,
his feet washed in the river by the Churches
St Mary Somerset and St Bride.

'There is no comfort, only resignation.'
At the memorial service in Drezzo
the mourners are outnumbered by bulbs.
God's banker is dead, though it's said his desk-lamp
shines like an angel on the top floor.
What is the faith that others live by?
Who came for him and why? Gold, speculation,

the unmaking of men made by the pledge that
anything they say so is true – solve it, you!

IV TAILING

If the clouds took up dust as they do water
they would rain the blood of those we loved.
London Bridge on a weekday morning,
the dark commuters gathered like filings,
and the one among them you must track
like a compass to the arms of Dominant House.
You're the last of the great biographers,
living in the echo of his footsteps,
the recording minister at his back.

Mist rises from the helipads and piers,
that Gothic swirl you've seen in old films,
when light comes off the pavement and the air's
a lift from Turner, implying all it hides.
They have found a second body under Blackfriars
    Bridge:
is that the way he means to take you,
through the dripping gullies and fur-halls,
a moth in the tenements of the mink trade,
a masked diver on the river's cobbled floor?

A blackbird dips down the alley, freak
of the City as foxes are and daffodils
or The Hatchet buried by Lippy Furs.
He is leading you into history,
past Zachary Gillam and the beavers
of Canada, whose tracking and trapping
concluded here as pelts in a warehouse,
the hunters contracted out before you,
their legacy the blood-rust of the Thames.

You have parked in the silence of hedgerow
and grass – bramble, foxglove, white convolvulus
with its spirals and bowls. Though you're concealed
there's a clear view of the lane and for an hour
only a beer-waggon has passed, with its corral
of rattling stock. But you're uneasy:
it's like that carriage on the night train,
tobacco smoke fresh in the corridor,
an invisible waiter at your back.

The names are in your ears of all the lost
adventurers, your peers, this one forthright,
that one sly, all of them now departed:
Taylor dying on the road from the airport,
Neilson who went mad on the underground,
Aspinall mauled, Boudin blown to bits –
lost, lost! In a sheet of flame you saw them
and you knew them all, the world's true masters,
its chief inquisitors, if the world but knew.

Then the car draws up and he steps towards you
with his carved walking-stick and broad-brimmed hat,
'Herr Mettich', in sandals (as you'd heard)
and a signet-ring sealing the handshake.
He takes his place beside the driving seat
in time for the afternoon eclipse,
the smoked window rising like a curtain
on his monologue, the only light a circle
in the dashboard glowing for cigarettes.

'Let me tell you what it is like to find
a man in our century. You have his name
but that's invented. No fixed address.
A chameleon of the identikit –

tall, short, dark, fair, moustached and clean-shaven.
Here's his photo, surely, on a picket-line
or is it here as ambassador to Rome?
No schoolfriend has seen him for fifteen years
and they ask for a report by next week.

'But I've his birthplace and the district,
fifty miles by a hundred. Popowo?
The yellowing map shows a fertile plain –
windmills, watermills, apiaries and hops,
a thousand hamlets tiny as pinheads . . .
But this Popowo, it's been abolished, clearly,
a landslide has carried it from the page.
I had to drive out one October dawn
under a sky shadowed with migrations,

'moss heavy on the trees, the roads slippery
with cattle-dung and elm-leaves, to the silence
of the spas. Here the people keep their heads down,
they hoard their secrets like fairy-rings
past Lisek, Fabianki, Swiatkowinza,
past barns, smallholdings and stagnant ponds,
until by chance comes a township, Popowo,
and a village doctor certain in his mind
Yes, a child of that name was born here.

'But he's alone: no one can recall the boy.
Days are squandered on the parish register
and nights in the company of cranks.
The black-dressed women washing linen
at the pump smirk over my impudence –
to ask such questions of the likes of them!
But, wait, the name's vaguely familiar,
a cousin who stayed during wartime – yes,
the family came from Chalin way, not here.

'Rain again, time passing through the drenched
    willows,
the wipers tocking like metronomes, until
at Chalin I learn – a miracle! –
Popowo's three miles south. *Another* Popowo,
where the chief clerk will personally
direct me to the "family seat", here
past the lime pit and the hardened cement-bags
to a bricked-up cowshed set among plums.
So this is all. He can see my disappointment –

'will I not join him for supper, it would
delight him to dine with me, a man of such
refinement and tact. But my interest
in that family, frankly he's surprised –
common folk who owned three hectares and a cow,
the father stirred up trouble, was caught stealing
newspapers from the big house – a rough lot,
certainly. They say the boy's now high in
government – should one believe it or not?

'At the school, a wooden mansion-house
long cobwebbed from disuse, the bearded caretaker
rises from her rocking-chair to furnish reports.
It might be said of almost anyone:
a diligent student of Class 1 B,
ran the 100 metres in 11.6,
walked about with his head bare, smoked a lot
and was a likeable sort of bully,
a good organizer, left in '61.

'Here it goes dark: his parents are dead,
no teacher or officer can recall him,
there's just the one letter to a schoolfriend,
with word of a job in engineering
and that he'd taken a flat near the Cathedral

for which he paid 800 zloty a month.
He is waiting in the shadows for history
to invent him, the 'little corporal',
remembered, if at all, as a card.

'So I returned to my superiors
and told them this man was a nonentity,
nobody to worry us in the least.
But that disruption at the shipyard?
His speech from the top of a telephone booth?
Put it down to his youthfulness.
Lenarciak, Suszek, Gwiazda, Nowicki –
these were the ones to keep an eye on,
this other just a ghost out of the sticks.

'You have guessed, of course, as you would have to:
this was Walesa, or soon to be,
there before my eyes yet wholly missing,
a face between nowhere and everywhere,
unfathomable as the workings of *Vlast*.
What hope for you, then, in your own quest?
Better write the history of a raincloud
than think one can ever know a man,
or tabulate the measures of his heart.

'I tell you this to save you disappointment.
I'll do my best to help: you must speak to Razumov,
who's made a clean breast, and to Kregraink.
Much beside the point can be accomplished.
But the task you have set yourself is hopeless,
a plot leading nowhere, a dark game
to distract you from knowledge, like the wind
through beeches keeping us with its promise
There is more to it, more to it, than this.'

VI THE PILLOW BOOK

You debate with a man from Penguin
evolution in a finch's beak.
You are full of haws and fossil-saws.
He prefers the explanation of God.
Around you mild and torpid monsters
settle for oblivion, more or less.
The celebrities have left for l'Escargot.
You're stuck with the passengers of alcohol,
taking their seats on its nightly express.

Then the tide recedes from the Galapagos
and you are left with her alone. *Eva,*
She smiles, and offers a hand to you,
and lets you fill her wineglass several times.
These publishers' parties – so dull, dull.
It was too obvious, but you're already
in the taxi, stepping north past Regent's Park
And Primrose Hill – to the glow of her bedstead,
her braceleted arm turning out the light.

How many evenings have ended like this:
to wake at dawn under a vaulted ceiling,
the sweet anonymities of one a.m.
reverting under the thin light to guilt,
loathing, fear of what a turned shoulder
will bring – though it brings, whether freckled or dark,
roughly the same: cracked lips, encumbered breath,
her dryness, yours. What was it kept you, then?
There was that nervousness at breakfast:

fresh orange-juice, white lies and reassurings.
She seemed impatient, as they always do,
showed you the door . . . which opened, though, on
   this:

the bed again, her dress on the floor like a shadow,
the green minutes of the digital clock
mounting inexorably as your breath.
She knows you'll be late for your appointment
but, wait, she must give you this – her Union,
To enter freely, come and go at will.

Weeks riffle past under an open window
like the pages of her Taoist guide.
What is your preference today? The tiger's tread?
The mountain goat facing a willow?
The feast of peonies or the pair of tongs?
These mysteries of cloud and rainfall,
like the passages no censor can excise:
'Stroking my hair, she moaned like Circe
As I buried my new beard between her thighs.'

Today, an hour with the Director
to present your returns. They are quite worthless
and he tosses his personalised golfball
with an air of disdain. *Let me be frank,*
old chap. There's been some pressure from above –
a deal with the Americans, it seems.
He takes his putter from the filing tray,
stooping over it as if to say grace.
I'd say another week is all you have.

Afterwards, at Gaston's, you are tempted
to confide. Her eyes across the table
appeal to you for candour, her hand
now rests in yours. But where would be the point?
It is not what you want with her anyway,
but to tip the chauffeur handsomely
and drive at once to some remote wood
behind the smoke of an official car . . .
Next day's a Friday and the August weekend:

you escape with her up the motorway,
its lamps curving their necks as if to sip,
swan-like, from the rushing passage of life,
or as arms might join above your head
for the bright arch of a wedding-dance.
In the hotel she takes four ribbons
from her bag: *One day I must start wearing them,*
but now, please, darling . . . The Prisoner
of Sex – it is a game she loves to play.

For hours you're awake with that special tiredness –
driving, the insoluble, and love.
Whose sweets were those in the glove compartment?
What did Karl mean by *the quieter room upstairs*?
Movement of arms by night – pairs of tail-lights
slipping down the road into another country,
or would it be by plane? She stirs beside you.
There are sounds across the mere like owls
or churchbells – it's impossible to say.

And there are wakenings more like wish-dreams
or death: to fight up from the oceanbed
and find her mouth on yours, her pouring hair
as if you'd stepped behind a waterfall,
her navel's mirror reflecting your own.
Breath matched by breath, you're like those mad twins
who speak each other's every word and thought,
the air still bristling with electricity
as she pulls on her silky green dress.

And so you tell her, since it seems she must know:
over cider, in the sunlit garden
of the Cockpit, she sits indifferent
through your narrative and this annoys you
so you tell her, very slowly, again.
The world should open up but there is only

the flutter of crisp-packets. Driving back
to London, buffeted by cross-winds
from juggernauts, it's as if she's failed some test.

VII NOBLESSE OBLIGE

Quels bons bras, quelle belle heure me rendront cette
région d'où viennent mes sommeils?

Rimbaud

This is the excitement that ends in pain.
Dark names stretch for you from their seedbed,
bronze statesmen harangue the crowded squares.
All week you've driven round the capital
in a blacked-out Volvo, testing the way.
What is this new air, ideas run up flagpoles,
the people pressing to some grand conclusion,
not to be restrained? It seems to lead
straight to disaster, or to lunch with Lascelles.

It was his job to let the Empire die,
but it dug in. Telegrams came from islands
it was thought were long since sold, their Morse
a sandpiper weeping over lost inlets
and strands, those northern coastlines like the hand
of a delegate pleading at the UN
Send out your forces and deliver us
from pain. We were at one with the sheep
and cormorant until the soldiers came.

Those cadences cost him his job. After
the bad reviews, the bayings for blood,
and then the blood in the bay to meet them,
he resigned, seeking consolation in
restaurants, where he'd amuse himself
in strategies with a wineglass and two forks

or the global policing of a melon.
These brought a navy made of toothpicks
cascading off Columbus's earth.

Today, years on, the world does not remember.
He's there in Bertorelli's, as they said
he would be, at the same corner-table,
with neither greeting nor smile. His drink's
Martini, since 'it reminds me of Martínez,
you know, de Campos, the Spanish general,
deposed for his leniency in Cuba.
I have become, you see, since my demise,
an expert in the scapegoats of Empire.

'They sent you, I know, for what I can tell
of the nation: *j'ai seul la clef de cette parade*.
Our leader dreams of bringing the Great back,
her Jerusalem's made of sterling,
her voice rings like a grocery-till, softened
with the pity she's hardened from the land.
Her grail's religious: coming from the flatlands
she dreams of death on a high green hill.
Nothing can countermand the Iron Will.

'And yet she's tapped the English heartland'
(this, as the waiters he's grown old among
scurry to the portholed door, which swings and swings
like an unfastened boom in a gale,
and the heaped promise of each silver dish
is carried to the white-beached archipelagos
then returns with its skeletal remains:
backbones, legbones, shoulderbones, brain –
and there are some still champing to be served)

'We are an island in love with the idea
of islands, of a marooned people,

helpless as seal-pups, crying for their lives.
Our hearts go out to them, we are authors
of a pastoral for the powerless,
protectorate of all shepherds and kelpers,
our Empire of Seaweed encircling the weak
on their windswept promontories of light.
So we succour and oppress, who might have slipped
from history unnoticed as the auk . . .'

But he's exhausted and drunk, the sentence
unfinished as he motions you to leave.
Your driver is waiting in Charlotte Street,
your journey back by tomorrow's parade-route
down Shaftesbury Avenue, the Strand and Ludgate
    Hill.
Scarlet hangings have gone up on the houses,
the new vision will be met with in tunes
whose stern injunction, culled from ancient hymn-
    books,
is to ransom the captive and *rejoice*.

At the Church of St-Andrew-by-the-Wardrobe
you ask the car to wait. The Observer's
behind you, the God long since renounced
is sulking still, and silent, but there are whispers
from the vestry, where the choir are arranging
their cassocks and hair. It's your image of trust –
the altar-stairs sloping through darkness,
children filing to the east window who sing
to perfection what they cannot understand.

And your report? Forehead to penthouse window,
you have your last view of the nation,
the river of a darkening capital
and its diamond clusters of self-love.
you could write now of good misdirected

and innocence betrayed, but the deadline has come,
only the foghorns wail like creatures from
prehistory: *Speak to us, who cannot see*
where we are going or know what is right.

VIII CANENS

You pick the children up at ten and drive them
east to Dunwich, a coastline they're too young
to remember, the city under the sea
where nothing of what happened remains.
You ask them (in passing) how their mother's been –
she was looking drawn, you thought, and they speak
of her tiredness and headaches. Right, past the church,
you follow the B road to the Bird Reserve,
a wind from Holland streaming through the hides.

The marrow in her bones was dissolved
by sadness and she wasted in air.
It's said the sources are always one
and the same. *Ovid, ibid* go a pair
of reedlings by the mill on Walberswick Marsh.
Your heart contracts to nothing as you consult
the drawing in your Child Ornithologists' Guide:
the male plump on freshwater molluscs,
the female sheltered under his rufous wing.

And her old letter, marking the entry
for *picus viridis*, the green one and its mate:
I believed in you. To survive as we did
early on, and then a second child and third:
I grew to think of it as an achievement.
It was your going away that changed it,
not the affairs themselves but the knowledge
I'd been living with an impostor.
It is all, you see, a question of trust.

This is how ghosts begin, the ash of memory,
white hawthorn and the mild-frothed river,
the milky shards she dug from the berberis
out of someone else's past, as if this mist
were the breath of the land's dead labourers,
the yeomen and marshmen, the husbands
and husbandmen, the sowers of seed
among flint and hummocks, gathering barley
while the North Sea cantered at their back.

And the cottage by the kalefields that year
after Finland: they had frozen all posts
and for a summer you lived there unoccupied
getting every detail by heart – the beads
she wore, the swing under the apple-tree,
the vine, the sandpit, and the hinged lid
of the nesting-box that was always going
to reveal some featherbedded circle
of happiness, but somehow never did.

You call them back to you, like a moorhen
with her bleeping chicks across the furry stream.
These reeds go down to where the beach begins,
a sandstone cliff-edge wearing into nothing,
less and less each year, as there is less and less
of her, a drained fen, a voice in a millstream
trying not to reproach, trying to keep
the children from its whispered briny song:
Yes, we were happy – but only for so long.

IX LET IT GO

Whose are the steps behind you in the hall
though the wet marble holds only your own?
Who is the son of straw? Whose warnings
carry in the wind, where the lamp breaks up

and the mirror can no longer hold its stare?
Your protégé is working at your desk.
There are skeletons in the filing tray.
They've acknowledged your review but consider
its conclusion *the product of an overstretched mind*.

Leaves rush towards you like peasants fleeing
a napalmed village of the East. It has
something to do with you – but what exactly?
When you slide the study window up
papers blow about the room and you must kneel
among them like somebody in mourning,
names staring up as if from gravestones
buried in the grass: Horovitz, Jeffares,
Casey, Lorne – faces you'd prefer to forget.

And the answer they want, would it be dull?
A name you rejected weeks ago?
Having the air of what you were supposed
to think? Or just less feasible than most?
The questions recede like hyacinths
then return with waxy clarity each dusk.
You're relieved you need no longer pursue them:
a plumb-line to the mud, a body
in the river with each fingernail extracted,
that's how the lost identities turn out.

'The conspiracy of our spacious song':
in your dream last night the elms along
the ministry drive seemed to part for you.
the passes had been passed, on a high floor
the final room was waiting, the answer
in a file marked NEVER TO BE OPENED.
It solves the world: there is a great party.
Eva, who is God, descends from the boardroom
to present you with a case of severed heads . . .

You see her next morning at the cottage
under the whish of an Icelandic wind.
The garage OPEN sign spins like a coin.
A fine spray is chiselled from rainbutts.
The swallows have gone from the outhouse,
painted warriors recalled to their wattle huts.
While she talks to you with emphasis
a white powder like cocaine or cow-parsley
trails its ashes from a bag of cement.

She is sorry to have been elusive –
she's been so busy, so very busy of late.
But this time spent apart has not been wasted.
She's come to recognise how things were
so much better before they became too intense
(yes, like standing at the edge of the town's
most exclusive party, not daring to go in).
What she means, to put it brutally, is
that *it's over, but we had best stay friends*.

She will have supper, please, you want her to
(for there's a question left to ask). Roast lamb,
red wine, something gingery with windfalls.
You'll choose the instant by the mantelpiece,
her face lit by the rush-burn of seasoned pine:
By the way, I met a friend of yours,
said he once worked with you in Milan . . .
And she admits it by not hearing
as she pulls you quickly to her one last time.

A solution of sorts, though the fields
deny it, returning a wintry blank.
The harvest tractor with gulls in its wake
has departed the way of all stubble,
the days are short, the last of the tourists gone.
Only the mole persists with its cottage industry,

there beneath the lawn could you but see it,
laying its sponge-roads and puffy veins,
its working life all channelled to one end.

There are no ends, though, and no answers, for this
is secrecy, whose art is to withhold
the logic it is richer not to know.
The word at large behind the berberis
cannot be caught, not quite. The padlocked gate
stays padlocked and we cannot trust our sense
of what was happening through its iron,
the child in search of a blackened tennis ball
who stumbled on a crossbow and a throat.

Now is the right time to surrender –
as in the weakening December light
one is suddenly thankful for the fourth stroke,
scone-time and the flicking on of headlamps:
at last one can drop all pretence of effort –
laying a path, dictating a letter,
or the task of deciding what we are
and where we come from – well, it's too late for that
and (anyway) no longer seems to count.

Your connection is waiting in the street.
One day he will ask to deliver a message
and the porter will 'forget' that he must not.
Aren't those his steps in the hallway now?
They have given him a key, then. His face,
there will be time and all time to observe
in passing its passing resemblance to your own.
And his voice, like a playback of your voice:
This is going to feel precisely like death.

Dark Glasses

And take upon 's the mystery of things
As if we were God's spies . . .
                              King Lear

The privacies of lace and leylandii.
The pseudonym to climb through like a trap-door.
The dark falling as you enter what was said
in the summer-house, behind the Chubb,
beyond the entryphone, inside the glass-topped wall.
What nestled through customs in a hub-cap.
What you must never mention to anyone.
For God's sake, Harry Lime, hold your tongue.

Or this other sort, let's-be-candid-please,
Big Mouth, the soul of indiscretion,
the gust that took the trellis clean away.
This Norfolk skyline, vast and open-hearted,
levels with its questioners, or seems to,
for though we left with a full confession
by the time we played the tape back that evening
it had reverted to a row of noughts.

Either way you come out none the wiser.
She is silky and elusive, returns
at twelve dripping beads from a broken necklace,
an accident, a little job for you
(a job to ignore the flush in her cheekbones
and the departure of a misted car).
And this – how you love it – is mystery,
wrapping itself around you like a bride.

But something cries out to be resolved.
The pen moves off with its search parties.
There are footlights on the dipped horizon,

118

as if the ones whose plot we are part of
were on the brim of coming clear. It's late
but they'll be here by nightfall, you know they will.
Just as you despair their red torches
flash through the dark like fluke late raspberries.

Notes

'The Kiss' (p. 3) was written around the time of the US bombing raid on Libya, which used British air-bases.

'On Sizewell Beach' (pp. 4–5): Though best known for its nuclear power station, the East Anglian coastal village of Sizewell also boasts a fine beach.

'Whinny Moor' (pp. 24–26): The epigraph comes from Richard Blakeborough's *Wit, Character, Folklore and Customs of the North Riding of Yorkshire* (1911); the legend also lies behind the anonymous 'Lyke Wake Dirge'.

'The Ballad of the Yorkshire Ripper' (pp. 33–47): For its narrative detail, the poem is much indebted to Gordon Burn's excellent study of Peter Sutcliffe, . . . *somebody's husband, somebody's son* . . . Some of the dialect in the poem was taken from Richard Blakeborough's book (above), which contains a glossary of four thousand words including 'baufy' (strong), 'belder' (to bellow as a bull), 'boggart' (a ghost), 'drabbletail' (a loose woman), 'flappysket' (ditto), 'fustilugs' (a weak fellow) , 'laikin' (a plaything) and 't'owerance' (the upper hand).

'Kindertotenlieder' (pp. 67–69): These free translations were commissioned by the theatre director Robert Lepage, for a musical drama based on Mahler's song-cycle. Mahler himself drew on five poems from more than four hundred written by the German Romantic poet and scholar Friedrich Rückert, two of whose children died from scarlet fever in 1834.

'Mist' (pp. 78–81): is narrated by a female twin.

'Xerox' (p. 93): Loosely inspired by the affair of Sara Tisdall, a young civil servant who leaked secret documents relating to the arrival of Cruise missiles in Britain.

'The Inquisitor' (pp. 94–117): A poem about British secrecy which attempts to recreate the atmosphere of a le Carré spy thriller and alludes to various episodes from the early 1980s, including the Falklands War, the rise of Lech Walesa and the death of 'God's banker', Roberto Calvi.